PREPARING FOR DISASTER

ENGINEERING SOLUTIONS FOR
EARTHQUAKES

JASON PORTERFIELD

rosen publishing's
rosen
central®

New York

Published in 2020 by The Rosen Publishing Group, Inc.
29 East 21st Street, New York, NY 10010

Copyright © 2020 by The Rosen Publishing Group, Inc.

First Edition

Library of Congress Cataloging-in-Publication Data

Names: Porterfield, Jason, author.
Title: Engineering solutions for earthquakes / Jason Porterfield.
Description: First edition. I New York: Rosen Publishing, 2020.
I Series: Preparing for disaster I Audience: Grades 5 to 8. I
Includes bibliographical references and index.
Identifiers: LCCN 2019007258I ISBN 9781725347762 (library
bound) I ISBN 9781725347755 (pbk.)
Subjects: LCSH: Earthquake engineering—Juvenile literature. I
Earthquake resistant design—Juvenile literature. I Earthquake
hazard analysis—Juvenile literature.
Classification: LCC TA654.6 .P68275 2020 I DDC 624.1/762—
dc23
LC record available at https://lccn.loc.gov/2019007258

Manufactured in the United States of America

On the cover: The steel sphere of the pendulum of the tuned mass
damper (TMD) in the Taipei 101 office tower in Taipei, Taiwan, is
18 feet (5.5 meters) in diameter. The TMD has reduced sways of
the building by nearly 40 percent, according to some estimates.

CONTENTS

Introduction

Earth's surface is always in motion, although people don't see it and they don't always feel it. During an earthquake, that motion can be felt. A small tremor may make the furniture shake a little or rattle pictures hanging on the wall. In bigger earthquakes, the motion may even be visible. The ground or the horizon may seem to jump up and down. You might hear a rumbling sound. It might be hard to stay on your feet. The earthquake you feel might have started hundreds of miles away.

The worst earthquakes sometimes cause serious damage. Buildings can collapse. Roads might buckle. Earthquakes can cause landslides or giant ocean waves called tsunamis to form. There's also a risk of fire caused by fallen power lines or broken gas lines. People can be seriously hurt or even killed. Sometimes smaller earthquakes called foreshocks happen before a big earthquake. Smaller earthquakes called aftershocks sometimes follow big earthquakes, causing more damage.

Earthquake engineering is a field of engineering that focuses on designing and building structures that are less likely to be damaged during earthquakes. The buildings that earthquake engineers design are meant to remain standing despite the violent motion of the ground. In addition to finding new ways to build structures, earthquake engineering also involves finding ways to make existing buildings stronger. Earthquake engineers often help town and city governments come up with rules for building safer structures.

The Transamerica Pyramid skyscraper in San Francisco, California, has several features that make it resistant to earthquakes. Its deep foundation and reinforced exterior walls allow it to move when the ground shakes. The X-braces, called trusses, above the first floor give it extra support.

Earthquake engineering involves various science, technology, engineering, and mathematics (STEM) subjects. Earthquake engineers need a solid understanding of these fields to design the strongest buildings possible. Through STEM methods, they can understand why Earth's surface moves, why some buildings are able to survive earthquakes, and how to make them stronger and safer for people. STEM subjects give them the background they need to make calculations, do research, and build models that can lead to new breakthroughs in earthquake engineering.

Preparing for the Big One

Earthquakes are often minor events. Many people have felt minor tremors caused by earthquakes. In some places, though, earthquakes are more likely to be big and dangerous. In those areas, earthquake engineering can improve building design so that fewer people are injured when the earth shakes.

Earthshaking Events

The constant motion of Earth is caused by the great forces at work beneath the surface. Earth is made up of three main layers. The outer layer is the crust. The mantle is directly below the crust. It is a layer of rock. Beneath the mantle is the third layer, the core.

The core is made up of two parts. The inner core is a solid mass, while the outer core is liquid and consists of melted iron, nickel, and other metals. Temperatures at the core reach more than 9,000 degrees Fahrenheit (5,000 degrees Celsius). The outer core spins around the inner core and generates heat. That heat rises up to the mantle, melting rock into a hot substance called magma. Magma then travels upward from the mantle and toward the crust in a process called convection. As the magma rises, it cools and returns to the mantle, where the heating and rising process takes place over and over.

The crust is made up of masses of rock called tectonic plates. They fit together imperfectly and are separated by large cracks called tectonic boundaries. Tectonic boundaries are not visible on the surface. Other cracks in Earth's crust are called faults. They are sometimes visible and often mark the site of seismic activity.

Convection causes Earth's tectonic plates to shift and move. The rising magma causes them to bump against one another, rise, fall, and grind together. Most of that movement happens very slowly. People seldom notice it is happening, even though it's going on all the time. This contact between plates can result in earthquakes. Earthquakes are typically very short. The longest last just a few minutes. Most are over within seconds.

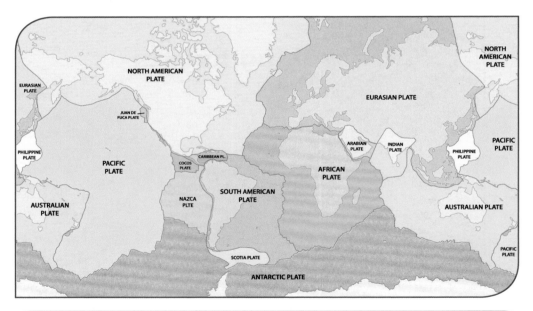

The tectonic plates that make up Earth's crust are in constant motion. Places near the points where tectonic plates meet tend to experience more seismic activity such as earthquakes.

The point where an earthquake begins is called the hypocenter, or focus. This starting point is where the tectonic plates shifted. This action creates friction that results in an earthquake. Damage caused by earthquakes is often worse at or near the epicenter. The epicenter is the point on Earth's surface directly above the focus. It's where the most violent shaking happens.

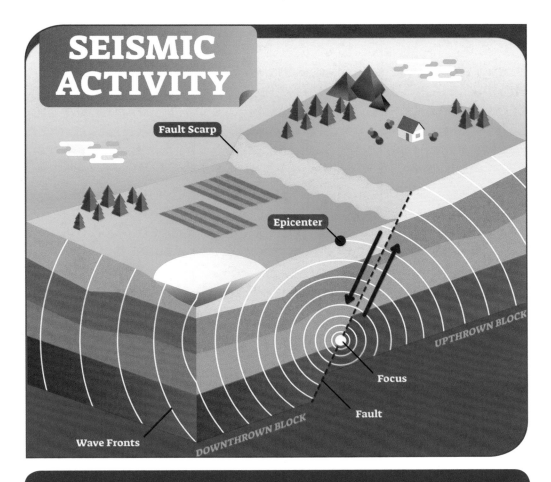

SEISMIC ACTIVITY

Fault Scarp

Epicenter

UPTHROWN BLOCK

Focus

Fault

DOWNTHROWN BLOCK

Wave Fronts

The focus of an earthquake is located underground. It sends energy outward, causing the ground to shake. The epicenter on the surface is located directly above the focus.

Seismic Wave Science

Earthquakes send out energy in the form of seismic waves, or shock waves. Seismic waves travel through the crust and shake soft materials such as clay in a process called liquefaction. Seismic waves react in different ways as they travel through various types of materials. Scientists measuring seismic waves can figure out what kind of material the waves are traveling through based on how they behave.

Two types of seismic waves shake the solid rock of Earth's crust. The first is called a body wave. Body waves move through the interior, or body, of Earth. The second is a surface wave, which moves near Earth's surface. Body waves are divided into two categories: primary (P waves) and secondary (S waves). P waves travel the fastest of the two and are called primary because they are the first waves that are recorded by seismographs. Seismographs record and measure the force of earthquakes. As P waves move, they expand and compress material in the same direction that they are traveling. Their movement is similar to the push and pull of a spring being squeezed from both sides and released.

S waves move more slowly than P waves and travel through the interior of Earth. They are called secondary because they are the second waves to be recorded by a seismograph. They travel in an up-and-down motion, but with an added ripple that causes the surface to rise and fall while also moving from side to side. P waves can move through water and air, but S waves can move only through solid rock. This property gives S waves more potentially destructive power than P waves.

Surface waves move across Earth's surface. They travel more slowly than body waves. They occur when the source of an earthquake is very close to the surface. They travel more slowly than S waves but can be far more destructive because they have more up-and-down motion to their side-to-side movement.

When the Shaking Stops

Earthquakes can cause significant changes to Earth's surface. Minor tremors that are barely felt by people can alter the landscape aboveground and below the surface.

Violent earthquakes are most likely to change an area's geography. The shaking caused by S waves, P waves, and surface waves can move stones and disturb soil. Landslides can occur as rocks and dirt are shaken loose and tumble down slopes. Fault lines might show up in cliffs or in the ground where shearing takes place. Some fault lines are located where tectonic plates meet, but they can occur in other places.

Earthquakes occurring beneath the ocean can cause massive and powerful waves called tsunamis. These waves sometimes hit land in coastal areas and cause a great deal of destruction. They can wipe away buildings and trees, sometimes killing hundreds or thousands of people.

Some powerful quakes generate seismic energy that sends water rushing onto land in powerful waves called tsunamis. Tsunamis sometimes cause widespread destruction in cities and towns near oceans.

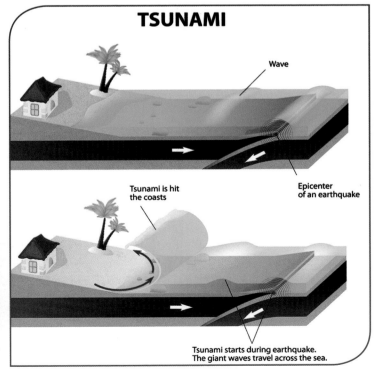

TSUNAMI

Wave

Epicenter of an earthquake

Tsunami is hit the coasts

Tsunami starts during earthquake. The giant waves travel across the sea.

The changes earthquakes bring to Earth's surface can be catastrophic. Earthquakes can also severely damage buildings. The side-to-side shaking can put a lot of pressure on structures, especially those that are taller than one story. In the worst outcomes, buildings can collapse.

Exploring Earthquake Engineering

Many different subjects are part of earthquake engineering. Seismology is the study of earthquakes, including their origin, movement, energy, and prediction. Geology is the study of Earth's history, its structure, what the planet is made of, and the forces that

The Loma Prieta Earthquake

In October 1989, a strong earthquake struck California. Its epicenter was near Loma Prieta Peak in the Santa Cruz Mountains, about 60 miles (97 kilometers) from San Francisco. According to the US Geological Survey (USGS), the earthquake caused sixty-three deaths, thousands of injuries, and between $6 billion and $10 billion in damages. Shocking television footage showed a freeway bridge collapse that resulted in forty-two deaths.

After the earthquake, California developed strong building codes. Old structures built of brick or cement blocks had to be strengthened. New rules were developed to make sure houses were securely fastened to their foundations. The state also began mapping areas where landslides were common and where the ground tended to soften during earthquakes in a process called liquefaction. These changes were important steps toward creating buildings that were safe.

act on it. Physics covers energy and its effect on matter, including physical structures such as buildings. Architecture is the field of designing and building structures like homes and skyscrapers. Various engineering disciplines such as mechanical engineering and structural engineering are part of earthquake engineering. They give earthquake engineers a solid understanding of how to plan and design sturdy and stable buildings, dams, roads, and other structures.

Earthquake engineers need a great deal of mathematics knowledge to carry out their work. They have to be able to calculate how much a building might sway in an earthquake and how much movement certain materials can withstand. Computer science is also essential for designing models of buildings for testing. The programs they use allow them to experiment with different designs and materials.

CHAPTER TWO

Planning for Disaster

Earthquake engineers try to lessen the damage earthquakes cause. They study the history of past earthquakes in an area to learn how often earthquakes happen there. This information helps them understand how strong the earthquakes tend to be there and the type of quakes that occur. They can figure out what kind of seismic waves result from those quakes. It also helps them figure out what buildings are likely to survive minor earthquakes with little or no damage. They can learn what structures can endure a major earthquake without collapsing.

Destruction and Damage

The motion of an earthquake can damage all types of buildings. Homes, stores, schools, and other structures that are firmly attached to the ground by their foundations are harmed as the ground moves.

In homes, quakes can cause foundations and walls to crack. Windows may break. Chimneys can crumble. Furniture may tip over. Walls and ceilings can fall down, sometimes making the entire building collapse.

There is more danger of earthquakes seriously damaging tall commercial buildings, such as office buildings in a city's downtown area. As the ground moves, buildings stay firmly rooted in place. Taller buildings are designed to sway during earthquakes. Shorter buildings are more at risk for damage because they don't move with the earthquake.

Other types of structures can also be damaged, such as roads, bridges, dams, and utilities. Earthquakes destabilize bridges and highway overpasses. Dam collapses are rare but can send massive amounts of water rushing out and cause floods.

The 1994 Northridge earthquake in California caused widespread destruction. The Federal Emergency Management Agency (FEMA) estimated that nearly 114,000 buildings were damaged.

Smart Designs

Earthquake engineers find ways of constructing buildings that make them less likely to collapse. Finding the right design does not always mean building a strong structure. An earthquake may eventually occur that is stronger than the building itself. Engineers study the materials used to build structures to learn what can best withstand an earthquake.

Earthquake engineers focus on designing buildings that follow "smart" design techniques. One major design change that emerged in the mid-1970s is to use a technique called ductile design. Ductile design is the practice of creating a building to move or deform in a particular way during an earthquake. The designs take into account that an earthquake is going to move the ground below the building.

Instead of the building staying solidly upright and potentially being damaged by the shaking, it is engineered to move or sway in a certain way. Steel is used in the frame because it is flexible enough to allow for some swaying. The building's vertical columns are designed to be strong so that it remains upright. The crossbeams are weaker, so they absorb more of the seismic waves from the quake. They may be damaged, but the supporting columns will likely remain in place.

One example of ductile design is to build a structure so that any damage caused by an earthquake is limited to certain parts of it. By using this kind of plan, engineers can control the amount of damage that is done to a building.

Engineers designed this skyscraper in Tokyo, Japan, to have a reinforced steel frame and ductile design. The thick vertical columns should enable it to sway during an earthquake without collapsing. The V-shaped supports are called dampers.

Studying Historical Data

Knowing about past seismic activity and earthquakes in a particular region helps earthquake engineers design earthquake-resistant buildings. Earthquake engineers study historical records that tell them about earlier earthquakes. Newspaper articles, diaries, and stories give engineers insight into how often earthquakes happen in a region. They learn how powerful earlier earthquakes have been and how much damage they caused. In many places, however, written records may go back just a couple hundred years. In other places, there might not be any written records of earthquakes.

The Pacific Earthquake Engineering Research Center (PEER) is located at the University of California–Berkeley. It is home to Strong Ground Motion Databases, which earthquake engineers use to learn about past earthquakes. They can use data from earthquakes such as the 1989 Loma Prieta earthquake to make engineering recommendations.

Earthquake engineers consult with seismologists and geologists to find out about earthquakes in a given region. Seismologists measure the strength of earthquakes. They estimate the strength of future quakes. Their work includes looking at rocks and soil to make their predictions. Geologists examine rocks beneath Earth's crust for evidence of past quakes, such as faults. Geologists sometimes dig trenches across or along faults to see what kind of changes earthquakes have caused. For example, trenches have been excavated for study along part of the large San Andreas Fault north of Los Angeles, California.

Geologists and seismologists study landforms that result from earthquakes in fault zones. Thousands of years of earthquakes in the same area can cause visible changes to the landscape, including certain types of valleys and ridges. Studying these landforms gives geologists clues about where earthquake epicenters are located and how often earthquakes occur. This study of changes to landscapes is called tectonic geomorphology. Landforms such as those around the Seattle Fault in Washington can show scientists how the landscape changed after earthquakes.

Measuring the Quake

Seismologists, geologists, and earthquake engineers use high-tech tools to study recent and historic earthquakes. The seismograph is the best-known device for recording earthquakes and measuring their strength. These sensitive machines detect vibrations constantly, drawing a continuous straight line on a roll of moving paper. Even minor vibrations can cause the line to jump, showing the force of the jolt. Scientists can see how strong a tremor was by the size of the spike it caused.

Earthquake strength is measured on a scale of one to ten on the Richter scale. The Richter scale measures the amount of energy released by the motion of rocks, with ten being the strongest. Most earthquakes measure at 2.5 or less and are not even felt. Strong earthquakes usually measure at 5.5 or higher.

Other scales measure earthquakes in different ways. The Modified Mercalli scale measures the intensity or amount of damage caused by earthquakes. It uses Roman numerals on a scale of I to XII. The Rossi-Forel scale was used during the late 1800s to measure seismic waves on a scale of I to X. Both scales rely on seismographs to show Earth's movement.

Tools to Study Changes in the Landscape

Sometimes geologists use airborne surveys carried out on small airplanes or with drones to find changes to the landscape caused by

Earthquakes and Structural Engineering Software

Earthquake engineers make changes to the digital model buildings they create and run simulated, or pretend, earthquakes many times. They take note of any improvements they make that reduce the damage. The models also help them see weak points in the buildings that may lead to a collapse or other serious damage.

Architects and engineers use structural engineering software to design strong buildings. Earthquake engineers apply these programs to figure out what improvements are most effective. Structural engineering software can test for ductile strength, for example. Earthquake engineers can swap out different types of supports and joints in the models they create with these software programs.

Bridges, dams, and other nonbuilding structures can be modeled with these programs. Factors such as the structure's weight are included in the models. Virtual stress tests can show how well a structure holds up in an earthquake and let the engineers know where their designs need improvement. If it shows a particular joint collapsing, for example, the engineers will look for ways to strengthen that joint. They can also investigate improved materials for the structure. In the end, digital models can help save time and lives.

earthquakes. Other tools that help show geologists what happened during an earthquake include 3D laser scanning.

Earthquake engineers use computer models to learn how an earthquake might change the land and what damage it might cause. They adjust the strength of the simulated earthquakes in these models to see how much stress existing buildings can endure and to figure out how strong to make new buildings.

Following a 6.1 magnitude earthquake in California on August 23, 2014, Richard M. Allen, director of the Berkeley Seismological Laboratory in California, points out areas that experienced aftershocks.

They use specialized software to create models of an area. These models include the geographic features of the surrounding land, any nearby faults, and the amount of seismic activity in the area. Earthquake engineers use computer models to see what happens to the land when there is an earthquake. They add existing buildings to the model to see how they behave when the ground shakes.

Before digital imaging became advanced enough to make realistic computer models possible, earthquake engineers used physical models. These scale models are still used to make improvements to structures and to see how changes to buildings might make them stronger. This information can be entered into the digital models to develop possible solutions.

Designing to the Threat

Buildings can be designed to withstand some earthquakes. However, even the strongest structures may be damaged in a strong quake. Weaker earthquakes can also cause massive amounts of damage, depending on how close the building is to the epicenter and what kinds of seismic waves are generated.

Strong Structures

Homes and other buildings bear their weight vertically, up and down in relation to the ground. In an earthquake, the ground can move up and down and side to side. Earthquake engineers need an understanding of the area's geography and a good grasp of architectural principles to design strong buildings.

The three main elements that go into building a structure that can survive an earthquake are its location, its design, and the materials used to make it. Technology, building materials, and the study of geology and seismology have advanced greatly. Today it is possible to construct buildings that are safer than those from the past.

Buildings that are three stories tall or shorter are often more vulnerable to damage in an earthquake. Taller buildings can sway during an earthquake. This ability gives them a way to release the energy that the shaking ground channels into them.

Every building in a city cannot be a skyscraper. Most are one, two, or three stories tall. They are stores, homes, office buildings, and businesses. Seismic engineers have to design better foundations and support elements for shorter buildings so that they can withstand an earthquake.

Heavily reinforced foundations give buildings the structural strength they need to remain standing. The brick, concrete, and wood that make up the building are anchored through strong frames. Supports called trusses give buildings more stability and prevent collapses. Trusses are made of wood or metal. They feature triangular shapes that help distribute weight more evenly so that one part of the structure isn't stressed more than others. The

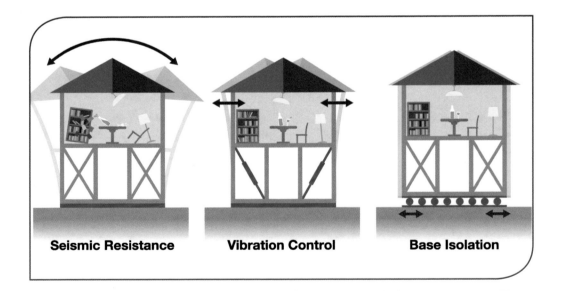

Seismic Resistance   **Vibration Control**   **Base Isolation**

Earthquake-resistant building designs protect structures from damage by minimizing the amount the building moves when it is shaken by an earthquake. These techniques include innovative foundation designs.

simplest trusses are a single triangle, though they come in many forms. In buildings, rows of trusses may be positioned to support ceilings, rooftops, and floors.

Steel plate shear walls are made up of sturdy steel plates that are thin and designed to flex. They are welded or bolted into place. These walls have been used in the United States since the 1970s to prevent building collapses.

A practice called base isolation changes the way buildings rest on foundations. Most building foundations sit right on the ground. In base isolation, the building foundation sits on a surface that is designed to move. Base isolation uses bearings made of rubber and steel as the surface on which the building sits. Some base isolation designs use rolling cylinders or springs instead of bearings. When the ground shakes, the bearings cause the building to move. The energy from the shaking is absorbed by the bearings or springs. This movement releases some of the energy of the earthquake without damaging the building's structure.

Tuned mass dampers (TMDs) are made for skyscrapers. They are large and heavy devices that work like pendulums. They help buildings sway during earthquakes without causing major damage. They are sometimes called harmonic absorbers. Usually they are located in the building's top stories. When winds or an earthquake cause the building to move in one direction, the TMD moves in the other direction to dampen the impact.

The Taipei 101 office tower in Taipei, Taiwan, has one of the world's most visible TMDs. Earthquakes are common in that part of the world, so many tall buildings have TMDs in their design. The 101-floor skyscraper has a steel pendulum that hangs from the ninety-second floor to the eighty-seventh floor. Its steel sphere weighs nearly 728 tons (660 metric tons) and can move 5 feet (1.5 meters) in any direction.

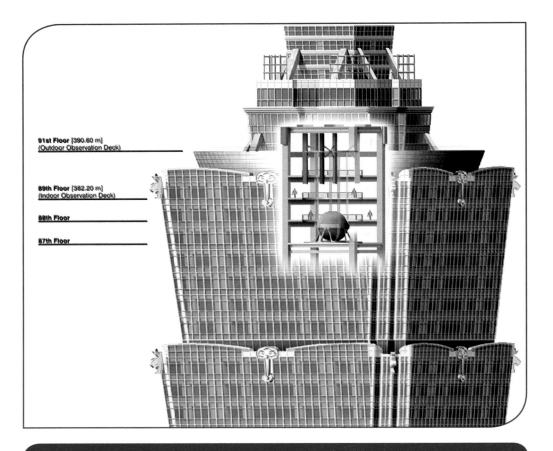

91st Floor [390.60 m]
(Outdoor Observation Deck)

89th Floor [382.20 m]
(Indoor Observation Deck)

88th Floor

87th Floor

Taipei 101, one of the world's tallest skyscrapers, stands close to a major fault line. Its massive TMD protects it from earthquakes and the strong winds common in the region.

The Right Height

Tall buildings are more at risk during long, slow earthquakes. They sway from side to side as seismic waves go through them. Shorter buildings move less in an earthquake but are at a greater risk of suffering major damage because they are not made to move as much as taller buildings. The longer the quake, the more they do sway.

The types of materials used in construction make a difference. Seismic engineers make decisions about materials based on a building's height. Steel and wood are more flexible than bricks, cement blocks, or unreinforced concrete. Bricks and blocks fracture easily under the physical stress caused by an earthquake. Concrete that is not supported by steel may break apart in an earthquake. Tall buildings are almost always built on steel frames, with reinforcements included to keep them in place.

Choosing the Right Site

Seismic waves travel through some of the materials of Earth's crust more easily than others. Most soil is made up of sediment—tiny particles of stone, plant matter, and other objects that have been reduced to tiny pieces over hundreds, thousands, or millions of years.

Resonant Frequencies

Earthquake engineers look at how buildings vibrate during earthquakes to figure out ways to make them sturdy enough to resist an earthquake. A building's vibrations are measured in its resonant frequency. The resonant frequency shows how much the building moves and how quickly this movement takes place.

High resonant frequencies can cause a building or other structure to become unstable, possibly leading to collapse. Taller buildings have a higher resonant frequency than shorter buildings, putting them at risk during earthquakes. By calculating a building's resonant frequency and studying models that simulate earthquakes, earthquake engineers make recommendations about materials and techniques that can lessen the risk of a collapse.

Places with solid bedrock—a layer of dense stone located beneath the sediment layer—are better building sites than areas with deep layers of soft soil. Bedrock absorbs seismic waves better than soil and vibrates less than soft sediment, making those areas more stable. Places with thin layers of sediment over bedrock are also more stable than those with thick layers.

Sediment quality in an earthquake-prone area also matters. Sandy soil can be unstable. It can cause a building to sway more in an earthquake than other soil types. Wetter soil found near waterways or in places with heavy rainfall can also be unstable.

People rescue items from the ruins of homes destroyed by soil liquefaction, which caused a tsunami. The tsunami hit Indonesia's Sulawsi Island in September 2018 after a 7.5 magnitude earthquake.

Buildings in such areas may sink in an earthquake. Sinking buildings often tilt to one side or sag at one corner. Foundations and walls have to carry added stress, and small structural problems like cracks become serious. Sinking increases the chance that the building will partially collapse or fall over.

Earthquake engineers study soil types before making their plans and recommendations. In some areas, the only places to build may have sandy soil or bedrock that is buried deep. In those cases, earthquake engineers make recommendations about what types of foundation and building materials to use. They also consider what heights and materials are best suited for surviving an earthquake in a particular area. If everything goes well, their recommendations are followed and safer buildings are constructed.

Building Safe Structures

Earthquake engineers direct the construction of new buildings based on the information they've gathered. They consider the types of soil present, the frequency of earthquakes in the past, and the damage done by earlier quakes. The destructive power and unpredictable nature of earthquakes make it impossible to design a building that's completely earthquake proof. Earthquake engineers work to make structures as safe as possible.

Earthquake-Resistant Structures

In places where earthquakes are common, such as Japan, Chile, and parts of the United States such as the West Coast and Alaska, rules called building codes direct what kind of buildings can be built. They may regulate building heights and what materials can be used in construction. A 1964 earthquake in Alaska led to strict building codes. Buildings throughout the state have to follow guidelines that call for beams and columns to be reinforced. When a 7.0 magnitude earthquake struck the Alaskan city of Anchorage in November 2018, most of the damage reported was minor. No deaths or serious injuries were reported.

A 7.0 magnitude earthquake that struck Anchorage, Alaska, on November 30, 2018, caused part of a road to collapse, trapping this vehicle. Strict construction guidelines protected buildings from major damage.

Building codes direct engineers and architects to design buildings that stand up to the strongest earthquakes likely to strike an area. Earthquakes can happen anywhere, but the risk is so low in some places that few precautions are required.

In the United States, two government agencies cooperate to create guidelines and regulations for buildings in places where strong earthquakes are common. The Federal Emergency Management Agency (FEMA) and the National Earthquake Hazards Reduction Program identify what parts of a building influence how it behaves during an earthquake. They identify several factors that go into making a building stronger. These factors are strength and stiffness, foundations, regularity, redundancy, and load paths.

Strength and stiffness deals with how the building moves from side to side and whether it is strong enough to remain stable while moving. A building's ductility is included in this strength and stiffness category. The foundations factor focuses on how the ground moves in an earthquake and how to best create a stable foundation.

Regularity has to do with how buildings sway during an earthquake. Earthquake engineers want to make sure the building does not move to one side more than the other, which places too much stress on that side and could cause a collapse.

Redundancy involves putting an entire system of safety measures in place in case one of the measures fails. Redundancy spreads the building's weight and mass out equally and thoroughly. Redundancy is expensive because it means using extra building materials. The costs are worth it when compared to rebuilding.

Buildings designed to withstand earthquakes have continuous load path. The load path extends from the building's highest point to the base of the foundation to evenly distribute its weight.

Load paths describe the ways the various parts of a building are linked together. They include the foundation, beams, joints, and trusses. Earthquake engineers want buildings to have a continuous load path. Each part supports itself, the previous part, and the load that connects to it. The connected parts spread the energy that seismic waves send throughout the building in a continuous path. Disconnected parts are more likely to move independently and destabilize the entire structure.

Following Building Codes

In the United States and in many other countries, building codes limit the types of frames and materials engineers can use in certain places. Building codes are generally decided by cities, towns, or counties. They describe the types of structures allowed, how they are built, and what materials can be used. Blueprints and detailed plans are submitted to the local government for approval. If there is a problem with the plans, they must be changed until they meet the rules. Builders can also apply for exceptions to allow their buildings to be constructed.

Governments in areas where earthquakes are common can be strict about building codes. Plans also must be approved for major home renovations. A homeowner might need to get a building permit for a job like putting up new cabinets.

Building inspectors follow up on new construction and renovations. They make sure the builders followed the plans and building regulations. Otherwise, the builder may have to make changes or start over. This process helps guarantee that every building is built to be safer in an earthquake.

Strengthening Dams and Bridges

Dams were among the earliest structures to be built with an eye toward earthquake safety. Starting in the 1930s, engineers made sure dams would stay stable. Standards have changed over time to make dams safer. Dams can become deformed by earthquakes. Earthquake engineers generally believe large dams can survive all but the very strongest earthquakes without major damage. Most of the weight dams have to support is distributed horizontally rather than vertically as is the case in a building.

Dams do not need to be flexible, but they need to be strong. Reinforced concrete is strengthened with steel used in dam construction. It has rods of steel called rebar inside it. The rebar pieces create a sort of cage inside the concrete. This cage makes the concrete more flexible by allowing it to crack and break without falling apart. Reinforced concrete is the most common building material used in new dams. Support structures called buttresses and berms help brace the dam in case an earthquake hits. Waterways called spillways release water behind the dam and relieve some of the horizontal pressure.

Bridges support a vertical load during an earthquake at either end. The bridge deck—the part of the bridge that cars, trains, and people pass over—is vulnerable to shaking that can cause a collapse. Earthquake engineers design bridges that are flexible enough to bend in an earthquake without breaking. Support columns are built with reinforced steel, and structural steel is used throughout bridges. In large

The Akashi Kaikyo Bridge in Kobe, Japan, took ten years to build. Trusses are visible below the roadway and in the support towers as part of the bridge's earthquake-resistant design.

bridges, towers and steel cables add more support. The Akashi Kaikyo Bridge connecting the Japanese city of Kobe to Awaji-shima Island was completed in 1998. Strong earthquakes are common in the area. The suspension bridge has trusses under the roadway and tuned mass dampers inside its support towers to help it stand up to quakes.

Tough Materials

Choosing the right materials makes a big difference when building earthquake-resistant structures. Strong frame designs and durable and flexible materials help smaller structures survive earthquakes. Engineers avoid using materials that fall apart under stress, such as bricks and concrete blocks. Steel and wood are better choices because they don't break easily. Reinforced concrete is particularly strong and is commonly used in new buildings.

Weighing Safety and Expense

Strong earthquakes can come out of nowhere. In places where major earthquakes are rare, it might not make sense to build structures to withstand the strongest quakes. Building materials can be expensive, especially reinforced concrete and steel. The expense may cause builders to think about putting up smaller buildings that use fewer construction materials. They may choose between making a building as strong as it can be or simply meeting the safety requirements.

Buildings with earthquake safeguards are costly but can protect lives. A strong earthquake that measured 6.0 on the Richter scale shook California in August 2014 in the Bay Area, near big cities such as San Francisco and Oakland, where buildings must meet high standards for surviving earthquakes. Some injuries and damaged buildings were reported, but there were no deaths.

Engineers design walls, foundations, and joints in smaller buildings to absorb the force of seismic waves. Engineers call the weight of buildings and the forces that act on them loads. The building's weight is a dead load. Forces like earthquakes, people moving around, and the wind are live loads. People and the things inside a building are vertical loads. Wind is a horizontal load. Earthquakes are both vertical and horizontal loads.

Houses and other smaller structures need a strong foundation to withstand an earthquake's horizontal and vertical loads. Concrete foundations should not have cracks. Reinforced concrete adds strength to new buildings and to those that are being rebuilt.

Some houses have a concrete slab as a foundation. Others have a concrete foundation going around the outer walls. Both home types need to be securely fastened to the foundation. Earthquakes can shake unsecured homes off their foundations, causing serious damage. Bolting the home's frame to the foundation keeps it stable if an earthquake occurs. Building regulations sometimes require houses to have reinforced structures called pony walls in place. These short walls support the home between the walls of the main foundation. They can be reinforced with braces and bolts.

Engineers consider the walls and roof when trying to build an earthquake-resistant home. Roofs should be made of light materials. Heavy roofs raise the center of a building's mass and makes it more likely to tip over. Heavy roofs also place more stress on the building's vertical load. Lightweight walls also help to make homes more stable during earthquakes.

Roads are easily damaged during earthquakes. Shaking ground causes road surfaces to crack. Landslides bury roads or cause them to collapse. Earthquake engineers use steel retaining walls to help protect roads from landslides in hilly areas like parts of California. The steel holds dirt and stone in place so it doesn't fall onto the road. Steel walls also support roads from below, with additional support from concrete or earth berms (raised banks).

Getting Ready for an Earthquake

Even strong structures can suffer serious damage during an earthquake. There are steps people can take to protect themselves during an earthquake. Quakes can be unpredictable. It's important to have a plan not only for the earthquake itself but also for any aftershocks that might follow and the damage they cause. It's possible to receive early warnings of earthquakes through the ShakeAlert system being developed by the US government for the West Coast. It can detect serious shaking quickly enough to notify people through a smartphone app so they can be ready.

Be Prepared

Earthquakes can happen anywhere, even though earthquakes large enough to be felt are fairly rare in many places. Everyone should know some basic steps that can be taken to stay as safe as possible if an earthquake occurs.

Have a plan—know where to go in your home during an earthquake. Choose a place in each room where nothing heavy is likely to fall on you. It's also a good idea to make sure heavy furniture and objects, like television sets, are secured to the wall so that they will be less likely to tip over. Heavy objects should be kept closer to the floor to prevent them from falling off shelves or other furniture.

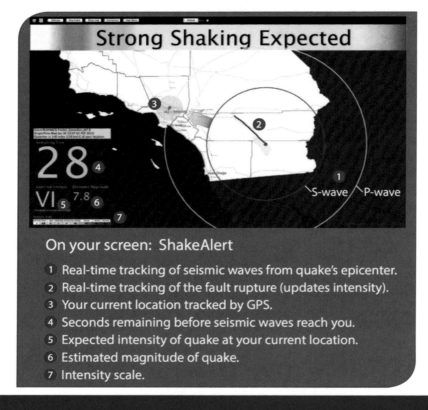

On your screen: ShakeAlert

1. Real-time tracking of seismic waves from quake's epicenter.
2. Real-time tracking of the fault rupture (updates intensity).
3. Your current location tracked by GPS.
4. Seconds remaining before seismic waves reach you.
5. Expected intensity of quake at your current location.
6. Estimated magnitude of quake.
7. Intensity scale.

The ShakeAlert app uses global positioning technology to pinpoint a user's location and track seismic waves. A countdown function shows users how much time they have to get to safety.

Be sure you know how to turn off the water and gas lines coming into your house. Water that's running in through broken pipes can cause serious damage to the home's structure. Gas escaping from broken lines can build up and possibly cause an explosion. Turning water and gas off at the place where they enter the building can reduce those risks.

Pack an earthquake kit with items that you might need in an emergency. The most basic earthquake kits might include bottled water, flashlights, batteries, a dust mask, a battery-operated radio, a first aid kit with some basic medical supplies, vitamins, and canned

When the Shaking Starts

There are some simple steps that you can take to stay safe when an earthquake starts.

- Drop down low and get under something strong, such as a bed, table, desk, or doorframe.

- Stay away from windows.

- Keep away from heavy furniture that can fall on you and hurt you.

- Stay inside until the shaking stops and it's safe to go out again.

- If you're outside, try to find a clear, open spot where nothing can fall on you, and get on the ground.

- Drivers should drive to a clear space and stop until the earthquake is over.

College students in Los Angeles, California, practice taking shelter under tables during an earthquake drill. The drill was part of an earthquake safety awareness event called the Great ShakeOut.

food. Remember to add some basic tools like a can opener, matches in a waterproof container, and a utility knife. Basic hygiene items like toilet paper and soap should go in as well. People also pack spare clothing, cash, and important documents like birth certificates in their earthquake kits. Food, water, and batteries should be replaced once a year so that they will be fresh and ready to use.

Your earthquake kit should be in a box or a sturdy bag that's easy to move. If possible, keep it in the room where you plan to go if an earthquake starts. Many people in cities where earthquakes are common have small earthquake kits that they keep with them at work.

Cleaning Up

It can be a relief to make it through an earthquake. Once the shaking stops, there may be many jobs to do. Cleaning up after a major earthquake can take time. Buildings should be checked for any problems that have developed, such as cracked foundations. Homes and other buildings that have been severely damaged may need to be torn down and rebuilt. People who were hurt in an earthquake need time to get better. Some survivors need counseling to help them recover from the trauma.

Homeowners and businesses with earthquake insurance can have some or all of the costs of repairs covered. Government agencies, such as FEMA, and disaster response organizations such as the American Red Cross and the Salvation Army can also help, especially by offering housing assistance for people who have lost their homes. For some people, it might be hard to decide whether to rebuild in the same city or to move to a place where earthquakes are less likely to occur.

A major earthquake often causes towns and cities to look at their building codes to see if changes need to be made. Earthquake engineers help by studying the damage caused, making recommendations, and working closely with builders. By applying earthquake engineering principles and STEM fundamentals, a city can be rebuilt with buildings that are more capable of making it through the next quake.

Glossary

aftershock A minor earthquake that follows a larger one. It can occur days or years after a big earthquake.

architecture The science and practice of designing a building.

berm A wall or mound that's often made of soil or sand and used to provide support to a dam, a roadway, or a larger wall.

building code A set of rules used by a city, town, or county to govern how buildings are constructed.

buttress A part of a building that sticks out from the rest to provide extra support and make it more stable.

earthquake A shaking of the ground that is caused by great forces and energy beneath Earth's surface.

epicenter The part of Earth's crust that is directly above the focus, the place beneath the surface where an earthquake originates.

excavate To dig away soil carefully to uncover something.

fault A break or crack in Earth's crust where blocks of crust on each side of the break move parallel to the break.

foreshock A small earthquake that comes before a large earthquake.

foundation The base on which a building rests.

geology The branch of science that studies Earth's history through its rocks.

horizontal Being parallel to the horizon.

joint In a building, a point where two beams or supports come together.

landslide Soil and rock that moves or slides down a cliff or mountain.

magma Melted rock found beneath Earth's crust.

prediction A statement that describes an event that is likely to happen in the future.

renovation The act of rebuilding or restoring a home or other building.

sediment A layer of sand, soil, and stones that is spread out over an area by natural forces.

seismic Relating to or caused by an earthquake.

seismic wave A wave of energy caused by an earthquake that moves along Earth's surface or through Earth's interior (body waves called P and S waves).

seismograph A device that detects and measures earthquakes.

tectonic plate A section of Earth's outer crust that is in constant motion.

trauma The state of being upset or emotional because of severe stress.

tremor A shaking or vibrating motion of the ground.

truss A triangular framework of posts and bracing that is usually used in roofs, bridges, and towers. A truss helps in distributing tension and weight evenly.

vertical In an upright or up-and-down position.

vibration The rapid back-and-forth or side-to-side movements of a body or substance.

For More Information

Canadian Association for Earthquake Engineering (CAEE)
Department of Civil Engineering
University of British Columbia
#2018—6250 Applied Science Lane
Vancouver, BC V6T 1Z4
Canada
Website: https://caee.ca
CAEE works to encourage earthquake engineering research and
    practices in Canada through partnerships with educators and
    professional societies.

Earthquake Engineering Research Institute
499 14th Street, Suite 220
Oakland, CA 94612
(510) 451-0905
Website: http://www.eeri.org
Facebook: @EERI.org
The Earthquake Engineering Research Institute works to reduce
    the dangers of earthquakes through earthquake engineering
    and developing meaningful ways to reduce risks.

Earthquakes Canada
Natural Resources Canada
7 Observatory Crescent
Ottawa, ON K1A 0Y3
Canda
(613) 995-5548
Website: http://www.earthquakescanada.nrcan.gc.ca//index-en.php
Twitter: @CanadaQuakes

Earthquakes Canada provides the latest news of recent earthquakes, tips on earthquake preparation, and information on historic earthquakes.

National Earthquake Hazards Reduction Program
Website: https://www.nehrp.gov
The National Earthquake Hazards Reduction Program is a partnership between several federal agencies with the goal of reducing earthquake vulnerabilities of facilities and systems.

Ready: Earthquakes
Website: https://www.ready.gov/earthquakes
This website is part of a US public service campaign to educate the American people about national disasters and to help them prepare for them. The website includes information on earthquakes, landslides and debris flow, and volcanoes, among other related subjects.

United States Geological Survey (USGS)
Earthquake Hazards Program
12201 Sunrise Valley Drive, MS 905
Reston, VA 20192
Website: https://earthquake.usgs.gov
Facebook: @USGeologicalSurvey
The USGS monitors and reports earthquakes, assesses hazards, and researches the causes and aftermath of quakes.

For Further Reading

Amson-Bradshaw, Georgia. *Earthquake Geo Facts.* New York, NY: Crabtree Publishing Company, 2018.

Bethea, Nikole B. *Civil Engineer* (Pogo: Stem Careers). Minneapolis, MN: Jump!, 2017.

Brooks, Susie. *Earthquakes and Volcanoes* (Where on Earth?). New York, NY: Rosen Publishing, 2017.

Cummings, Judy Dodge. *Earth, Wind, Fire, and Rain: Real Tales of Temperamental Elements.* White River Junction, VT: Nomad Press, 2018.

Higgins, Nadia. *Natural Disasters through Infographics* (Super Science Infographics). Minneapolis, MN: Lerner Publications, 2018.

Kolls, Harry, and Steve Mills. *Design a Skyscraper* (You Do the Math). Irvine, CA: QEB Publishing, 2015.

Malizzia, Diana. *A Visual Guide to Volcanoes and Earthquakes* (A Visual Exploration of Science). New York, NY: Rosen Publishing, 2018.

Owings, Lisa. *What Protects Us During Natural Disasters?* (Engineering Keeps Us Safe). Minneapolis, MN: Lerner Publications, 2015.

Parks, Peggy J. *Great Jobs in Engineering* (Great Jobs). San Diego, CA: ReferencePoint Press, 2019.

Spilsbury, Louise, and Richard Spilsbury. *Earthquake Shatters Country* (Earth Under Attack!). New York, NY: Gareth Stevens Publishing, 2018.

Waeschle, Amy. *Daring Earthquake Rescues* (Rescued!). North Mankato, MN: Capstone Press, 2018.

Wagstaffe, Johanna. *Fault Lines: Understanding the Power of Earthquakes*. Victoria, BC: Orca Book Publishers, 2017.

Bibliography

Brocher, T. M., R. A. Page, P. H. Stauffer, and J. W. Hendley II. "Progress Toward a Safer Future Since the 1989 Loma Prieta Earthquake." US Geological Survey Fact Sheet 2014-3092. https://pubs.usgs.gov/fs/2014/3092.

California Department of Conservation. "Loma Prieta Earthquake—20th Anniversary (1989–2009)." Retrieved January 20, 2019. https://www.conservation.ca.gov/cgs /Pages/Earthquakes/loma_prieta.aspx.

Chen, W. F., and E. M. Lui, eds. *Earthquake Engineering for Structural Design*. Boca Raton, FL: Taylor & Francis, 2006.

Cooper, James D. "World's Longest Suspension Bridge Opens in Japan." Public Roads, July/August 1998. https://www.fhwa .dot.gov/publications/publicroads/98julaug/worlds.cfm.

D'Oro, Rachel, and Mark Thiessen. "Strict Building Codes Helped Anchorage Withstand Quake." Associated Press, December 1, 2018. https://www.apnews .com/018a78f7cfb646b8a6653766a953cacd.

Folger, Peter. "The National Earthquake Hazards Reduction Program (Issues in Brief)." Washington, D.C.: Congressional Research Office, 2018.

Fountain, Henry. *The Great Quake*. New York, NY: Crown, 2017.

Hickok, Kimberly. "Tons of Major Quakes Have Rattled the World Recently. Does That Mean Anything?" Live Science, August 23, 2018. https://www.livescience.com/63412-california-big -quake.html.

Los Angeles Times staff. "Concrete Buildings, Earthquake Safety, and You." *Los Angeles Times*, October 12, 2013. http:// timelines.latimes.com/l-quake-danger-which-buildings-are-risk.

Miles, Kathryn. *Quakeland: On the Road to America's Next Devastating Earthquake*. New York, NY: Dutton, 2017.

Nabhan, David. *Earthquake Prediction: Dawn of the New Seismology*. New York, NY: Skyhorse Publishing, 2017.

National Earthquake Hazards Reduction Program. "Recommended Seismic Provisions for New Buildings and Other Structures." Washington, DC: Federal Emergency Management Agency, 2015.

Prager, Ellen J. *Furious Earth*. New York, NY: McGraw-Hill, 2000.

Robinson, A. G. *Earth-Shattering Events: Earthquakes, Nations, and Civilization*. New York, NY: Thames & Hudson, 2016.

Robinson, Andrew. *Earth Shock*. New York, NY: Thames & Hudson, 2002.

Somers, Peter. "Recommended Simplified Provisions for Seismic Design Category B Buildings." Washington, DC: Federal Emergency Management Agency, 2017.

Sparks, Dana. "About the California Building Codes & Earthquakes." *San Francisco Chronicle*, December 11, 2018. https://homeguides.sfgate.com/california-building-codes -earthquakes-2592.html.

Údias-Vallina, Augustín. *Principles of Seismology*. Cambridge, UK: Cambridge University Press, 2018.

Index

About the Author

Jason Porterfield is an author and journalist living in Chicago, Illinois. He has written several STEM-related titles, including *Becoming a Quality Assurance Engineer* (Tech Track: Building Your Career in IT); *Robots, Cyborgs, and Androids* (Sci-Fi or STEM?); and *Robots, Jobs, and You* (The Promise and Perils of Technology). He enjoys learning about Earth's geology by exploring caves and studying the rocks and minerals he collects.

Photo Credits

Cover Sunwand24/Shutterstock.com; cover hexagons (left to right) Nattapong Wongloungud/EyeEm/Getty Images, CHUYN/E+/Getty Images, D-Keine/E+/Getty Images, © iStockphoto.com/Alessandro Rizzo, john finney photography/Moment/Getty Images, Fernando Ojeda/EyeEm/Getty Images; pp. 4-5 (background) Warchi/iStock/Getty Images; p. 5 (inset) photo.ua/Shutterstock.com; p. 8 Rainer Lesniewski/Shutterstock.com; p. 9 Vector Mine/Shutterstock.com; p. 11 Designua/Shutterstock.com; p. 15 FEMA/Wikimedia Commons/File:FEMA-13711-Photograph by FEMA News Photo taken on 01-17-1994 in California.jpg/CC0; p. 16 Shigemi Okano/Shutterstock.com; pp. 20, 29 © AP Images; p. 22 metamorworks/Shutterstock.com; p. 24 Someformofhuman/Wikimedia Commons/File:Taipei 101 Tuned Mass Damper.png/CC BY-SA 3.0; p. 26 Kyodo News/Getty Images; p. 30 Naeblys/Shutterstock.com; p. 32 Matt Roberts/Getty Images; p. 36 USGS/Wikimedia Commons/File:ShakeAlert.jpg/CC0; p. 37 Al Seib/Los Angeles Times/Getty Images; cover and interior pages graphic elements © iStockphoto.com/koto_feja (spiral design), Ralf Hiemisch/Getty Images (dot pattern).

Design and Layout: Tahara Anderson; Senior Editor: Kathy Kuhtz Campbell; Photo Researcher: Sherri Jackson.